THE
WOMAN
OF

Faith

Leading a life full of hope

J O L A N D A   K A H O R O

WESTBOW
P R E S S®
A DIVISION OF THOMAS NELSON
& ZONDERVAN

WestBow Press books may be ordered through
booksellers or by contacting:

WestBow Press
A Division of Thomas Nelson & Zondervan
1663 Liberty Drive
Bloomington, IN 47403
www.westbowpress.com
844-714-3454

Scripture taken from the King James Version of the Bible.

ISBN: 978-1-6642-1411-8 (sc)
ISBN: 978-1-6642-1410-1 (e)

Print information available on the last page.

WestBow Press rev. date: 12/01/2020

CHAPTER 1

The Story of Hope

JOHN 11:20

Most of you probably have known and heard this story before. Everybody preaches it all the time. The story about Lazarus and how he was dead for four days and Jesus raised him up. However, today, I will not be writing that much about Lazarus. I know you must be thinking - if so, what are you going to be writing about?

I will be talking about the sisters of Lazarus, Mary and Martha. I like the story of Lazarus - one of the greatest manifestations of God's miracle ever. Yet, as I was reading this particular Scripture, the Holy Spirit moved my eyes back to the top of the page to John 11:20. He asked me, "Why do you think Martha ran to Jesus?" I said I did not really know. For a month and a half, that question had stayed with me. I kept asking God why Martha ran to Jesus and Mary stayed.

Well, this is what the Holy Spirit told me: Martha had hope and she knew who Jesus was - she caught a revelation that Mary and the rest of the people of Bethany did not catch. *The Bible said, "When Martha, as soon as she heard that Jesus was coming, she ran, went and met him, but Mary stayed in the house." (John 11:20)kjv.*

Hope provokes faith and faith provokes God to do a miracle for you. Why do I say that? You see, the Bible said it is impossible to please God without faith;

> *But without faith it is impossible to please him: for he that cometh to God must believe that he is, and that he is a rewarder of them that diligently seek him. (Hebrews 11:6)*

> *Now faith is the substance of thing <u>hoped for</u>, the evidence of things not seen. (Hebrews 11:1)*

Without hope you cannot have faith. You see the definition of **hope** is **a feeling of expectation and desire for a certain thing to happen.** Let's say, for example, you want something good to happen, like finding that perfect job that suits you. You get to the interview and you are expecting to get that job. Now that is **HOPE.**

On the other hand, **faith** is **complete trust or confidence in someone or something**. You have hope that you will get this job because you believe that you have what it takes, or that you meet the requirements to be hired. Maybe you have faith in your resume, or your talking skills, or your training.

What I am trying to tell you is that hope and faith go hand in hand; and Martha had both. Why do I say that? When she heard that Jesus was coming, she ran. The Bible said that Jesus was not even in town yet; he was on his way but has not gained entry. Martha did not even want to wait until he gets to town. She just had to meet him halfway... Are you thinking what I am thinking? Maybe God wants us to meet him halfway; before he can enter into our lives, solve our situation, and resurrect the dead, stinky things that we bury like marriages, finances or relationships. You see the Bible said in *Isaiah 55:6, "Seek the LORD while he may be found; call on him while he is near."* The Lord wants us to seek him. You might be asking, but how do I seek the Lord? My answer is **run to Jesus,** like Martha. Cry on these feet. Pour out your pain and your sins, and he will heal you. Jesus said in *Mathew 11:28-30, "Come to me, all of you who are weary and carry heavy burdens, and I will give you rest. Take my yoke upon you and learn from me, for I am gentle and humble in heart, and you will find rest for your soul."*

That is what Martha did. She ran to Jesus and poured out how she felt at his feet. Let's all be honest. We all have blamed God one way or the other for not showing up when we needed him the most, just like Martha's first words in ***John 11:21, "Then said Martha unto Jesus, Lord, if thou has been here, my brother had not died."***

I will be honest. I sometimes feel just like Martha, that God had abandoned me when I am most in need of his help, comfort and love. There are times when we are all living for God, answering God's calling upon our lives. Then, troubles and tests come, and we say, "God, I have been holy and righteous, so why is this happening to me?" The first thought that comes to mind is that God has forgotten about us. However, that is far from the truth. Let me tell you why I say so. You see, if you look back to the beginning of that Scripture, Jesus had a prior conversation concerning Martha's issue - her brother Lazarus - with his disciples.

*"And after that he said unto them,
our friend Lazarus sleepeth; but
I go, that I may awake him out of
sleep." (John 11:11)*

Jesus knew everything before it even happened. He knew that Lazarus was going to die. God knows everything about us. Nothing about us is a shock to God. The Bible said he never sleeps nor slumbers. Nothing that is happening to you is a shock to God, not even one. He knows you so well, that he gives you battles that will shape and mold you into the person he knows he created you to be.

However, my question is: why did Jesus wait for Lazarus to die?

- Faith has to be tested
- God's glory has to manifest

What do I mean by these two things? I will explain to you what I mean and how these two keys play an important role in trusting God and staying hopeful in the storms of life, as a woman and a man of God.

YOUR FAITH HAS TO BE TESTED

What do I mean by "faith has to be tested"? You see, in the same Scripture, John 11 stated that Jesus loved Lazarus.

> **"Now Jesus loved Martha, and her sister, and Lazarus." (John 11:5)**

So if he loved them, why did he allow such a tragic and painful situation to happen to them? Or think about yourself, why does God allow pain, hurt, confusion and struggles in your life even after you have given your life to Christ Jesus our Saviour?

God has to test our faithfulness before he can perform a miracle in our lives. Deuteronomy 8 is a very good example of how the children of Israel were warned by God. He explained to them why he made them go through such a long journey in the wilderness. Scripture stated that God was doing it to humble them so they can learn to rely on him completely.

> *"And thou shalt remember all the way which the LORD thy God led thee these forty years in the wilderness, to humble thee, and to prove thee, to know what was in thine heart, whether thou wouldest keep his commandments, or no."*
> *(Deuteronomy 8:2)*

God tests you to humble you, to position you for your miracle. He does it through the testing of your faith. You can act all Christ-like outside and fool the people around you; but you can never fool God because God does not see like man does, he looks into your heart.

> **"But the LORD said unto Samuel, Look not on his countenance, or on the height of his stature; because I have refused him: for the LORD seeth not as man seeth; for man looketh on the outward appearance, but the LORD looketh on the heart." (1 Samuel 16:7)**

I am not saying "You are a bad person" or "Your heart is not right, that's why you are facing what you are facing." Sometimes, he just wants to test you because he wants to promote you to a higher level. He needs you well equipped and ready to take on a new promotion in your life. Sometimes, we pray and ask for big things. However, first, God needs to position us so we will be able to handle what he will bless us with.

GOD'S GLORY HAS TO MANIFEST

Our God is a glory God. Every time he wants his glory to manifest in us, he brings troubles. He makes sure only he can solve this trouble; that a miracle is needed as he shows up and turns the impossible into possible; and then, he is glorified.

Sometimes, he is glorified through you. You see, when you are facing all kinds of storms, you pray and you fast. Yet, sometimes, God does not show up right away. God is a timing God. God is always on time. Some troubles are intentional. Your struggles are intentional. Your singleness is intentional. Your battles are intentional. Even your pain is intentional. God wants to prove your enemies wrong. Whatever they do to you, whatever they throw at you, God sees it all. When your enemies are mocking you - asking you where your God is - let God answer your prayers. You pray all the time but God does not hear you, maybe you go to the wrong church, or God is just quiet, and the list goes on. However, delay does not mean denial for God. It means, "I am about to do something big for you, my child, and I need you to separate the leaves from the branch; so you will know who is for you and who is against you." Then, he shows up like an earthquake, changes your story and shuts the mouth of your enemy. Finally, God is glorified.

I am sure Martha felt the same way. People were probably talking about them - about how their friend, Jesus, the man who healed many and raised the dead, did not come and heal Lazarus. He left him to die, even after Martha and Mary sent a message to Jesus that their brother was sick. However, all of it was not true. Jesus knew what was going on. He still loved them. He still loves you.

The Scripture that confused me was **John 11:4.** When Jesus heard that Lazarus was sick, he said, ***"This sickness is not unto death, but for the glory of God, that the Son of God might be glorified thereby."*** Like I said, God's glory has to manifest.

So Jesus knew what was going on with Lazarus and chose to ignore? I thought that at first, but when I found out the revelation about God's glory, I understood right at that moment. God had to be glorified through Jesus via this great miracle of all times. God will be glorified through you as well.

CHAPTER 2

Believing is Everything

WHY IS IT IMPORTANT
TO BELIEVE GOD?

Believing is the sign of faith. Faith activates the hope in our souls. Martha had that in her soul, I learned, while reading the Scripture about this amazing woman who went beyond her pain to discover something supernatural and experience God's power that was in Jesus Christ. Martha provoked the supernatural to manifest in the natural. The moment Martha said yes - I believe - was the key for God to move on her behalf. The Bible said in **John 11:25-27,**

> *"Jesus said to her, "I am the resurrection and the life. The one who believes in me will live, even though they die; and whoever lives by believing in me will never die. Do you believe this?" "Yes, Lord," she replied, "I believe that you are the Messiah, the Son of God, who is to come into the world.""*

God is asking you the same question today... **do you believe?**

Do you believe you are free, redeemed and restored? Do you believe in Jesus and the power of his resurrection? Do you believe that he is able to do exceedingly, abundantly and beyond what you ask or think? **(Ephesians 3:20)**

Let me tell you some things that I know about our God. He is faithful. He never fails. He is always on time. I myself have experienced this amazing God in my life. Only through your faith can you see the goodness of God. God has never failed me before and always with me **(Mathew 28:21)**. Your problems or how you feel can never change God. His love is everlasting. His mercies are plenteous. All the people said, "Amen!"

Martha experienced the amazing grace of God because she said "Yes, Jesus I believe in you." Sometimes, we say we believe and we have faith in God but do we really? You will know when trouble comes. When trouble comes, it separates infant from man. What I mean is we find out who we really trust, God or the world. Believing in God alone is not enough. Believe also in Jesus. Most people, even Christians, have their opinion of who Jesus is. Many do not want to believe he is the Son of God, who now is our Lord. Like Jesus said, **"You believe in God, believe also in me." (John 14:1)** *Anyways, he is the way to God. He is all in all.*

THERE IS POWER IN
BELIEVING IN GOD

Faith is never faith until you start believing. That's why the Bible said, **"Whatever you ask, believe that you have received it and you will have it." (Mathew 12:22)**

Throughout Scriptures, Jesus encouraged people to believe and have faith. He became agitated whenever people did not have faith. I remember the Scripture when he and his disciples were caught in a storm. Jesus was sound asleep while the disciples were fearful for their lives. When he woke up, he said to them, ***"Oh, you of little faith, why are you afraid?" (Mathew 8:26)*** God wants you to trust in him, to have confidence in him above all. Like in Joshua 1:6, God encouraged Joshua to be strong and courageous. You see, God has not given us the spirit of fear. Fear is not in God's DNA. If fear steps into your life, it is the enemy, not God. The enemy cripples you with fear until you are completely paralyzed. However, that is not how God created you to be. In you there is a courageous man and woman.

WHO YOU RUN TO AND WHERE YOU RUN MAKE A WHOLE LOT DIFFERENCE

Two things that define you and your problems:

- Who you run to in trouble will determine the outcome
- Where you run determines who you trust

Who you run to

Who you run to when faced with trouble will determine the outcome of the situation. Take a look at the woman of hope, Martha. Martha wanted a different outcome. She wanted a better outcome. She did not want the familiar outcome. Hence, she had to run to someone that will give her a different outcome. You see, in the eyes of men, Lazarus was gone. He was no more. However, in the eyes of God, Lazarus was taking a nap, a long but restful nap. What is my point? My point is that when we see with natural eyes, we see natural things, how they are in the natural. However, when we look with the eyes of God, we will see differently. Martha wanted to see with the eyes of God. Therefore, she ran to the person that will show her through the eyes of God. We call that faith. Remember, we walk by faith, not by sight. Friends, who do you run to when faced with trouble? Learn to go on your knees and look to the author and finisher of your faith. He got you covered. Trust in him. The Bible said in **Proverbs 3:5, "Trust in the LORD with all your heart and lean not on your own understanding; in all your ways acknowledge him, and he will make your paths straight."** I love this verse, a very good verse to meditate on every day. One that said all that needs to be said about trust.

Where you run to

Where you run to shows who you trust. Girls, if you meet a new guy, you will run right to your bestie and tell her every detail. If you had a great day at work, you would want to talk about it with your spouse. The same can be said when you have had a rough day at work. You will want to share everything with the one you trust, because you know they care and they will listen. It is even better when you run to God because he will listen. God will do a miracle because God cares for you. When you go through the Bible from the Old Testament to the New Testament, trust is mentioned 181 times or more. When you read the stories of men and women who carried big tasks for God, it was trust and faith that led them to experience God's power to carry those tasks. Moses had to trust God to help him deliver the people of Israel out of Egypt. Through trust and obedience, God's power was manifested. What more can I say? Joshua had to do the same thing. Esther had to trust God to deliver the Jews from being murdered through fasting and prayer. The list goes on. All these people I just mentioned had to learn to run to God and seek his help, and they succeeded. My question is where do you run to when faced with trouble?

CHAPTER 3

But I Know that Even Now

Martha did not look at her circumstances as how it looked in the natural. She knew her God. She knew he was bigger than her circumstances. This Scripture moved me:

> *(John 11:22) "But I know that even now God will give you whatever you ask."*

You see, Martha did not go and live her past. She lived in her now. She did not go

Jolanda Kahoro

and complain about what God did not do for her yesterday. She could have lived in her past and blame God for not coming on time and healing her brother when he should have in the first place. She lived in the **now.** She believed in the God of the now. I would say this is a whole new level of faith. Take this example of a woman who had faith to the end. She did not say, "God did not come on time so I am not going to believe anymore, and I am not going to talk to Jesus anymore because he has failed me". Instead, she took her faith to a whole new level:

- *She ran to Jesus: which is a sign of "I am not giving up yet."*
- *She showed her pain to Jesus: which is the sign of "I am hurt, but I still trust you."*

- ***But even now I know:*** *which is a sign that says "I still trust God can do it for me even now."*

Martha worked her miracle to life. My spiritual father **Prophet Kofi Danso** *was right after all, miracles are worked for and not prayed for;* **DPKD.**

Martha's faith moved God to do a miracle for her family. Jesus knew that Martha carried the faith that will move God to use Jesus to perform a miracle in the town of Bethany. God is moved by faith. Again, without faith, it is impossible to please God. I am sure Martha's faith pleased God so much that he could not wait to do a miracle for her. Such faith provoked God. Are you provoking God to do a miracle for you or are you delaying it? Increase your faith, work your miracle and learn to trust God no matter the situation you are in, good or bad. God is still God. God never changes. *(Hebrews 13:8) "Jesus Christ is the same yesterday, today and forever."* In Matthew 13:58, the Bible said Jesus was not able to do any miracle in his own town because of their unbelief. This means God only works with believers. God does not respond to your unbelief, so believing is a sign of faith.

Let's be honest. How many of you today can look at Mary and Martha's failing relationship and their hopeless lives and decide to still believe in God? Can you still get on your knees and say to Jesus, "Even now I know You can still do it, not my will but your will be done?" The Bible said, *"Count it all joy when you face all kinds of trails; because you know that the testing of your faith produces steadfastness." (James 1:2-3)*

THE GOD OF THE NOW

Our God is a God of the now. God does not look at the past. God looks at the now. Martha was able to catch a revelation that you are about to catch as well. Do not get too caught up in the past that you cannot see the present opportunity that God has put in front of you. We pay so much attention to what we fail to accomplish that we do not see what God is doing with our failure. If you allow pain to control you, it will blind your faith. Pain will steal your hope and turn you bitter. You will miss other opportunities that God has placed in front of you if you are not careful. Take time to heal your past and stand in the now. See how God will transform your life. In the promises of God, the word of God always says **I will,** the word of God does not say, I "could have. *Martha connected to the*

Jolanda Kahoro

now and saw how far it took her. Connect to your now and see how far it can take you.

God's ways are not your ways

God's ways are very different from our ways. When you give your life to Jesus Christ, you are basically saying, "Lead my soul, God, I am all yours." As believers, we give our souls to Jesus and still we want to lead ourselves. When you trust God with your life, you come to find out that even when God does not give you what you pray for, you do not become disappointed at all because you know there is a reason behind the **no**. At this stage, you would have had a strong foundation. When a "no" comes or a delay from God happens, you will not throw a tantrum like the baby in Christ you used to be. Instead, you will act like a mature man or woman that God has created you to be. You will know God

30

very well, that his ways are always higher and best. Little did Martha know that Jesus was not late to fix her situation. He was just right on time. God is going to be just right on time for you too.

God thoughts are not your thoughts

The way you think is not how God thinks. Stop trying to think for God. We always want to assume why God has not responded to our prayers or requests (thoughts like, *"maybe I am still a sinner"* and *"maybe I am not good enough"*). Stop, stop, stop right there. God said in **Jeremiah 29:11, *"For I know the thoughts that I think toward you, saith the LORD, thoughts of peace, and not of evil, to give you an expected end."*** Simply, the way God thinks is not the way you think. Ask him what he thinks about you and find out what he says about you and your destiny.

We make our own desires our first priority that we never stop to think about what God wants for us or desires for us. Before you go on with your goals, take the time to sit with God and find out what he says.

Seek God

- Fast and pray
- Meditate on his word
- Have time alone with God to hear him clearly

• CHAPTER 4 •

Our Pain and our Faith

DO NOT LET PAIN STOP YOU

Trouble will come. Grief will come. Pain will come. Tribulation will come. However, do not let it affect your relationship with your heavenly Father. Jesus promised us peace but he never said that there will be no trouble. He warned us in *John 16:33, "In this world, you will have trouble but be of good cheer, I have overcome the world."* Mary is a very good example of what pain can do to a person. Luke 10:38-4 tells us how Mary used to sit at the feet of Jesus and listen to what he was teaching. What happened to that faith she had back then in the book of Luke? Pain had overshadowed her faith. Mary stayed, why? If you really look at that Scripture, it is tricky. When she heard that Jesus was on his way to Bethany, Martha ran but Mary stayed. Does that mean Mary also heard that Jesus was coming and chose to have stayed? Because if she did not hear the news of his impending arrival, I am sure the Bible would have stated otherwise. My guess is she indeed heard about Jesus like her sister Martha did, but she chose to stay behind because pain and discouragement took over.

Her pain was so much that when the people that were with her in the house saw her ran outside, they thought she was going to cry some more at her brother's grave. She rose up with sorrow and pain. I am not saying she was wrong. All I am saying is do not let your pain blind your faith.

GIVING UP SHOULD
NOT BE AN OPTION

A lot of us give up as soon as we do not see any results in our walk with Christ. My question is: is it really that we do not see results that we give up or is it because it does not go our way that we give up? A lot of people I had come across with gave up on God because God will not answer their prayers. Then, sadly, they came to a conclusion that God does not love them or he does not exist. If you follow God with conditions, you become manipulative towards God. God will not follow your conditions because there are times when what we pray for is not what God wants for us. It is not his will for us. The only way to see true blessings and favor in your life is to trust no matter what. Job is one of the men in the Bible who showed us what trust is like. Job lost everything: his children, his possessions and his honour. Yet, he went on to say, ***"Thou he slay me, yet will I trust him." (Job 13:15)*** Job trusted God. This is what trust is all about: it is not your will, nor your way, but putting your complete trust in God at all times. In **Psalms 62:8**, David said ***"Trust in him at all times, ye people pour out your hearts before him; God is a refuge for us."*** Like Martha did in John 11:20, when you trust in Jesus, hope is born. When hope is born, faith is activated. When faith is activated, you start to walk in supernatural power. A little glimpse of hope in Martha's life activated faith. That faith caused Martha to see the supernatural power of God's glory to manifest right in front of her eyes. She could hug her brother again - something she did not think possible. What an amazing grace!

FAITH THE SIZE OF A MUSTARD SEED IS ENOUGH

A mustard seed is tiny, only about 1 to 2 millimeter's. So small, yet it can grow into a huge tree. Jesus compared faith to a mustard seed. What he meant is even that little faith you have can manifest God's power to work on your behalf. Look at Martha. I am sure her faith was not big either but it manifests God's power to resurrect her brother. Jesus said in *Matthew 17:20, "If you have faith as little as a mustard seed, and say to this mountain be moved from here to there, and it shall be so; nothing will be impossible."*

God does not require a lot from you, just a little faith to move mountains in your life.

We all have faith in us. You just need to activate it.

Martha was broken and hurting but she still carried her mustard seed faith. She decided to plant it in God and it brought forth a miracle. No matter how small your faith is, it can still move a mountain in your life. Martha made up her mind that the little hope that she had left, she would run to Jesus and plant it in him.

Plant your seed in the right soil so you can see the fruits. There is nothing that you give to Jesus that he does not multiply. He prayed over bread and fish. They multiplied and fed a multitude of people (**Mathew 13:13-21).**

Jesus spoke in parable about a farmer who sowed seeds in the ground. Not all the seeds he sowed fell on the same ground **(Mathew 13:1-23)**. My point is that little faith or hope you have, make sure it falls on good ground. Make up your mind like Martha and sow your seed in Jesus. You did all you know but the world failed you. Your loved one failed you. Now you do not know who you must sow in. Sow in Jesus. He never fail.